THE FOUR SEASONS

THE
FOUR
SEASONS

A Play in two Parts

by

ARNOLD WESKER

JONATHAN CAPE
THIRTY BEDFORD SQUARE
LONDON

FIRST PUBLISHED 1966
REPRINTED 1971
© 1966 BY ARNOLD WESKER

Jonathan Cape Ltd, 30 Bedford Square, London WC1

ISBN 0 224 61075 9

Permission to quote from 'Lament' in *Collected Poems* by Dylan Thomas has been granted by the Trustees for the Copyrights of the late Dylan Thomas, and to J. M. Dent Ltd.

The music for Adam's song was arranged by Wilfrid Joseph.

PRINTED IN GREAT BRITAIN BY
WILLIAM LEWIS (PRINTERS) LTD, LONDON & TONBRIDGE
BOUND BY G. AND J. KITKAT LTD, LONDON

The first presentation of this play was given at the Belgrade Theatre, Coventry, on August 24th, 1965, with ALAN BATES as Adam and DIANE CILENTO as Beatrice. The sets were designed by ZBYNEK KOLAR, of the Army Theatre, Prague.

Dedicate

e romantic revolution
aria Rosa, Edmundo, Abelardo, Bertina
e innocent revolution
del, Camilo, Che, Pepe
e undergraduate revolutionaries
grid, Jose, Rebecca, Ugo
e amateurs administrators
ario, Calvert, Maria Elena, Fernando
e soldiers who sing
d the singers who guard
rtocarrero, Milian, George, Chiki
e sea by my window, the Sierra Maestra
e Varadero beach and the peso that is not worth a dollar
senneh, Enky, Rine, Candela
e glorious mess you've made for
e children who read and the waiters who learn
aydee Santamaria, Mirian, Pablo, Teresa

ot because of the slogans which soon no one will believe
ut because you've turned the barracks into schools

ot because of the traitors you've killed to the whine of righteous words

ut because of the seeds of forgiveness I know you have

ot because you would ever win if the big fight came
ut because you are not afraid that you might lose

o Cuba

Characters are

Adam
and
Beatrice

Part One

WINTER

Two young people enter a deserted house. They have cases of belongings with them.

The house is furnished with a mixture of antiques which, if they have any beauty, have only the beauty that accompanies neglected and sad things; and of plain furniture assembled, perhaps, by hand.

It is evening. His name is ADAM, *her name is* BEATRICE.

They could be between thirty and thirty-five years old.

ADAM. We're safe, it's all right, no one lives here. You don't think anywhere is safe do you?

I used to pass it every morning until one day I just couldn't resist and came in. God knows who'd own a house like this and then leave it.

Won't you even say if you like it? Say 'I like it.' Just those three words. Or 'I don't like it' or 'Let's leave.' Or give a deep sigh or smile. Won't you even sit down? You will if I bring you a chair, won't you? I can see you'll do nothing unless I prepare it for you.

Right, then for the first weeks I'll prepare everything for you. Make your food, your bed, warm you. Just for the first weeks.

Won't you even say three words? Try. Please. Say 'I – ' (*He waits*) 'like' (*He waits*) 'it.'

(*No response.*)

Sit then.

(*He pulls out a chair, dusts it and gently leads her to sit down.*)

Listen to that wind. Are you cold? I must put a new pane in that window tomorrow, or sometime. It is cold.

(*He looks around for an object to stuff in the empty frame. An old piece of sacking serves the purpose.*

Then he rummages in his case and draws out two blankets.)

Here. Warm. The first thing, always, is to be warm.

(He places one over her legs.)

Invalid. You are an invalid aren't you? You're beautiful also.

(BEATRICE closes her eyes, and sleeps. ADAM watches her for a long while.

He raises his hand and is about to touch her face.)

No. I won't touch you. Will you believe that? You must believe something. I wonder why sad faces are such lovely faces? Sleep, I won't touch you.

Such a lovely face. A face I could love. Even 'love' again. But I won't, lovely lady. Not love again. Not all that again. I'll give you human warmth but not human love. Not that again. Not all those old, familiar patterns of betrayal again, those reproaches. And you know them, don't you? I can tell as you sleep, from the lines round your eyes, you know them.

What would you say if you were awake just now? You'd say 'Are you afraid? Are you afraid of love?' And I'd say 'Yes, I'm afraid of love.' And you'd chide me, gently, call me coward. 'Those who are afraid to die, die a thousand times,' you'd say. And then I'd feel foolish and mean for holding back and I'd give. Give and give and give because every part of me aches to give.

No. Not again. Not all that again.

(BEATRICE wakes with a start.)

Bad dreams? They'll pass. I'll get wood for a fire. *(He moves, then turns back.)* Won't you say three words, just three?

(She remains silent and he leaves to gather some fuel.

She watches him to the door and for a long time stares after him.

2

Soon her head moves back again to look at the room.
Its sadness, its desolation, its cold reach into her. She is
crying.

Her blanket falls to the ground and she slides from the
chair to her knees, hugging the blanket to her.

ADAM *returns and stands by the door. He makes no move*
towards her.)

Get up. Beatrice, get up. Beatrice? Beatrice?

(He continues to chant her name, calling it, rather; urging,
gently, 'Beatrice, Beatrice, Beatrice.' Till, slowly, she
returns to the chair.

He moves to pick up the blanket and again lays it over her
legs.)

'Ye hasten to the dead? What seek ye there?' Do you
know those lines? Shelley. 'Ye hasten to the dead? What
seek ye there?'

(Now he lays the fire and lights it.)

Do you know I hardly know the sound of your voice? Is
it high or shrill? Mellow? Contralto? Tiny? I used to sit in
buses or trains and gaze at beautiful girls, and sometimes
they'd smile at me and I'd smile back and see every virtue
in their faces: gentleness, understanding, passion – and
then they'd speak, and everything I'd imagined about
them would shatter. How can lovely eyes have ugly voices
I wonder? Is your soul on your lips or in your eyes?
I don't know. Do you? Answer me that. Just that. Just
that. Say 'eyes' or 'lips', say. Or point. Do that, even.
Just point. Not even that?

Listen to the wood crackling. Smell it?

(She breathes in, slowly, slightly.)

Again, Beatrice, again.

(Again she breathes in, this time a deeper breath.)

Again, can you do it again?

(*She turns her head away; for his foolish persistence she has,
for the moment, dismissed him. He can understand nothing.*)
You think I don't understand, don't you? How I recognize
that look. The female dismissing the male. I can read your
eyes; no will, no wish to talk, no wish to move, to act, I
can read them. But can you read mine? Can't you see pain
in my eyes? Can't you guess it? Do you imagine I'd bring
you here, commit a whole year to you if I understood
nothing? Do you?

And yet, I'm a fool to ask. Forgive me.

Look, even the gas is on. (*He has turned on a stove.*) Isn't
it miraculous? (*He moves out of sight.*) AND THE WATER
TOO. (*Sound of water; he returns.*) We have fire and water.

(*He picks up the other blanket and moves to a chair in which
he sits, covering his legs, like her, and gazes at her.*)
Isn't it miraculous?

(*There is a long pause as the two sit. The days are passing,
the weeks, even.*)

(ADAM *rises suddenly from the chair and throws his blanket
down. It is morning.*)

ADAM. Gentleness is no good, I can see that. It just produces
more self-pity doesn't it?

(*He now busies himself with putting the room to order,
wiping away dust and cobwebs.*)

Look at you. Call yourself a woman? Your face is falling
apart with self-pity. You don't impress me with your
silence. I could do that, what you're doing, sitting there,
silent, morbid, lifeless. I could do that. You're even enjoying it aren't you? How lovely it is, suffering. All the world
is against you isn't it? Eh? All the world is a fool, and

you're alone and suffering. (*Mockingly.*) 'I'm alone. I'm born alone. We're all, all born alone.' Lovely. Splendid. Very satisfying. Suffering. Lovely, lovely suffering.

And yet I know. Why should I mock you? I know. I've also loved and been loved. But I destroyed that love. Why should I mock you?

You were right to dismiss me, we don't really know each other. Even though I look at you and see myself and try to guess yet – I don't know. Poor girl, we grieve for ourselves don't we?

But look, I live! I go on. Beatrice, I go on.

You don't believe me do you? She doesn't believe me. (*Writes this in the dust on a piece of furniture.*)

She – doesn't – believe – me.

(*He pretends to hear this next question from someone far off, cupping his ears.*)

Eh? What's that? Why doesn't she believe me? Why? (*Shouts back answer.*) BECAUSE YOU NEVER RE-COVER, NEVER. That's why.

Why don't we ever recover, Beatrice? Won't you answer that even?

Not even that you'll answer. Poor Beatrice. I mean that; poor, poor Beatrice. Poor Adam.

(*He moves to the window, listlessly surveying the bleak outside.*)

Beatrice, what colour is the wind?

Perhaps we should wait for the winter to pass.

(*They are really living in their own hells.*
The days are passing, the weeks, even.)

(ADAM *sings to her.*
It is a late evening.)

5

ADAM.   'The wind doth blow tonight my love,
        And a few small drops of rain;
        I never had but one true love;
        In cold grave she was lain.

        'I'll do as much for my true-love
        As any young man may;
        I'll sit and mourn all at her grave
        For a twelvemonth and a day.'

(*He recites the rest.*)
        ' 'Tis down in yonder garden green,
        Love, where we used to walk.
        The finest flower that e'er was seen
        Is withered to a stalk.

        'The stalk is withered dry, my love,
        So will our hearts decay.
        So make yourself content, my love,
        Till Death calls you away.'

See, even I have become morbid. If we stay together many more months do you think we'll just fall apart? Disintegrate with misery? Waste away? Look, if I stand here, by the window, and you sit there, day after day, quite still, do you think God would take pity on us and turn us to stone for ever and ever? Let's try. You, there; me, here. Quite still. Don't move now.

(*They freeze for a long, long time. Then –*)
Have you ever known a God as unobliging as ours?

(BEATRICE *smiles.* ADAM *moves quickly to face her.*)
You smiled. I caught you smiling, don't deny it. I did, didn't I? For that – a present. Today a special treat.

(ADAM *moves quickly to his case and withdraws a hairbrush. Then he stands behind* BEATRICE *and takes the pins from her hair till a lovely mane falls behind her.*
    He gently brushes it.)

See what we give to the people we comfort? The tested gestures of love. Those very things that we know have given pleasure to others before. Does that offend you? But what's the alternative? Immobility? Silence? I used to remain silent because it seemed to me that all my thoughts should be kept for one person only. To know more than one person was to betray them, I thought. You know, it was my silence – more than anything else – that made my wife miserable. That, more than anything else. But what could I say? What could I tell her? Every ounce of passion was claimed, given elsewhere.

But she had her glory, my wife, her retribution. One day a young man came from another country to be our guest. He had eyes like an uncertain child in a strange and festive room and he laughed with deep pleasure at everything he saw. You could show him nothing and take him nowhere that didn't offer him delight. And gradually I saw my wife unfold from her misery as she gathered her heart and her senses to carry him from one place to another. All the secret corners of our own past she revealed to him and he held her hand and blessed her kindness as they walked over bridges and looked into the river and ate in friendly restaurants – the tested gestures of love. For two weeks she grew to the size she once was and abandoned her children, her home and my infidelity. Every ounce of *her* passion was now claimed, given elsewhere. And as I lay in bed till the early hours, waiting for her return, no one at my side, imagining the tenderness and passions they were sharing then, just then, at that precise and very moment – I clenched my teeth and cried 'justice' to myself. Justice, justice, justice! To know more than one person is to betray them.

But who remains silent for ever? And now, because there is neither wife nor mistress I sing to you, speak poetry to you and brush your hair. I'm honest at least. Or is the sight of a man being honest a pathetic sight? Most women think it is don't they?

You have lovely hair. How nice to take a woman's hair in your hands and be able to say that: Beatrice, you have lovely hair.

(*He moves to kneel in front of her.*)

Beatrice, you have lovely hands. Beatrice, you have lovely eyes, and lips and skin. Do you forgive me for saying it? You don't know what it means to be able to say those things to a woman. You only know that a woman needs to hear them said but you don't know the pain that grows in a man who is struck dumb with no one to say them to, you don't know that do you? No, I will not touch you, but will you let me look at you? I could cry when I look at you. But then – they would only be tears for myself.

Do you think the winter will ever pass?

(*He lays his head in her lap, fatigued. His eyes close, he breathes deeply. She regards him for some seconds, then slowly raises her hand to his head. It has cost her to do this and after the effort her body relaxes. She too closes her eyes. The night passes, the days, the weeks, even. Till –*)

SPRING

A long ray of sunshine cuts through the room. It is a morning.
    BEATRICE *opens her eyes.*
    At first she is startled, then she realizes where she is. Very gently she raises ADAM's *head, takes her blanket to cushion him where her lap was, slides off the chair and moves out of the house.*
    In her absence the sunlight grows stronger and the room is witness to winter passing.
    Soon she returns and in her hands is a large bunch of bluebells. These she lays upon the still-sleeping ADAM *till he is decorated from head to foot, and on the last flower he awakes.*

ADAM. I've not had such a beautiful thing done to me since –

BEATRICE. See what we give to the people we comfort? The tested gestures of love.

ADAM. You garlanded your lover with bluebells?

BEATRICE. Every morning.

ADAM. And at night?

BEATRICE. I oiled my skin with a different scent.

ADAM. You worshipped him?

BEATRICE. What else do you do to the man you love?

ADAM. Some women make their lovers wait and offer love as though it were a favour.

BEATRICE. Your sluts and your whores do that, but not your women, not your real women.

ADAM. Then you're a rare woman.

    Now what is it? Your face has fallen again.

BEATRICE. So many people have once considered me a rare woman.

ADAM. But aren't you? You seem so sure, so confident, even your silence was so confident. Look at you. Soft

9

skin, proud cheeks, penetrating eyes – one knows. Too penetrating perhaps, too intelligent – but sad also, and such weariness, such haunting, wordly weariness. One knows.

BEATRICE. Aren't you frightened?

ADAM. Oh yes, but of course. I feel I want to rush away and change my clothes, they're all wrong and ill shaped. The clothes I have belong to a city clerk or an estate agent, now I feel they should belong to a prince. I feel clumsy and careless. The brush I brushed your hair with is made of nylon and I feel now that it should be made of bristle. My gloves are resin and I feel they should be leather. And the way you hold your head and glance at me, even that makes me doubt the thoughts I've always thought. I'm frightened, intimidated, but what should I do – you are a rare woman.

There, your face has fallen again. Is it something I've said? Are we going to return to silence again? It is something I've said, isn't it?

BEATRICE. You must not –

ADAM. Must not what?

BEATRICE. You must not –

ADAM. What? What? What must I not?

BEATRICE. Gently, Adam, gently. You must allow me –

ADAM. – all the world! All the world I'll allow you. How can I refuse you? Look at that sun, look at that morning, it's a morning for offerings. All the world I'll offer you, only ask. Just ask.

My mother used to ask me, 'Do you love me?' and I'd say, 'Yes!' And then she'd say, 'How much?' and I'd say, 'Sixpence' and she'd say, 'Is that all?' And I'd say, 'Two and sixpence.' 'No more?' she'd ask. And I'd say, 'All the world, then. I love you all the world all the world all the world all the world.'

What more can I offer you? Fourpence for a cup of tea? The cream off the milk? I give it you, and the sun and this whole morning.

BEATRICE. You'll drown me with words.

ADAM. That's the way I feel, what can I do? Do I embarrass you?

BEATRICE. No.

ADAM. Do I overwhelm you?

BEATRICE. No.

ADAM. Then thank God for me and stop complaining – that's the way I feel. After a winter of silence that's the way I feel. Stop complaining.

(*There is a terrible sound of crashing from outside.*

ADAM goes to see what has happened. Soon he returns with a fallen drainpipe, and some broken tree-branches.)

ADAM. Spring comes and it's time to repair the damages of winter.

(*He looks round the room and, on seeing a broken hat-stand, places the drainpipe over it and puts the branches into the drainpipe. There is now a 'tree' in the room which, when the walls later move aside, becomes a tree in the country scene.*)

Are you fit?

BEATRICE. Your command is my wish.

ADAM. I see. It's to be like that is it? I'm always suspicious of a woman's offer of obedience. Still, I'll risk it, even again. You want me to give the orders? I'll give them. First of all – food. Prepare food. Can you cook?

BEATRICE. I can try.

(*She goes to the stove and shows him the inside.*)

Will this do?

ADAM. It smells of Italy – what is it? You can cook.

BEATRICE. Why should you imagine I can't cook, or run a household? You mistake my silence for inability.

ADAM. You're cheating. Let's have no cheating. Obedience and false modesties – there's no time.

BEATRICE. Come now, if I have false modesty you have false innocence.

ADAM. Aaaaaah!

BEATRICE. Did that hurt?

ADAM. Yes. Did you mean it to hurt?

BEATRICE. I'm sorry. Old reflexes.

ADAM. But it came so easily, so quickly.

BEATRICE. I've developed the habit. I'm sorry.

ADAM. You put me on guard.

BEATRICE. Please – don't be on guard.

(ADAM *relents and prepares the table with a great flourish.*
A splendid white cloth is produced and cutlery and crockery
drawn out from the sideboard.)

ADAM. I'm ravenous. I could eat a hundred sheep and drink a hundred tankards of beer. Do you know how many stones I turfed out of that garden this morning?

BEATRICE. How many?

ADAM. Guess.

BEATRICE. How can I guess?

ADAM. Guess, say a number.

BEATRICE. Don't play games, Adam.

ADAM. Yes – play games. Why not? Doesn't pessimism ever lose its attraction for you? Do you prefer morbidity? Play, I'm tired of being morbid. Play. Let the cold go.

BEATRICE. Cold?

ADAM. Cold, whatever it is –

BEATRICE. Ice.

ADAM. There's a difference?

BEATRICE. You don't know the difference?

(*Pause.*)

ADAM. Still, play.

BEATRICE. Twenty?

ADAM. No.

BEATRICE. Fifty?

ADAM. No.

BEATRICE. Five hundred, then.

ADAM. One thousand, one hundred and ninety-seven and a half.

BEATRICE. A half?

ADAM. There was a little cracked stone, all blue with cold. I buried it again.

BEATRICE. I'm afraid the village didn't have much of a selection of wines, there was only this.

ADAM. Stop apologizing.

BEATRICE. And these, look, there was a little antique shop, I picked them up cheaply.

ADAM. Serviette rings! We're building a home! Silver?

BEATRICE. Georgian too.

ADAM. You know?

BEATRICE. Quite cheap, I promise you. The poor man didn't really know what they were.

ADAM. So of course you had to buy serviettes.

BEATRICE. Are you angry?

ADAM. Angry?

BEATRICE. At my extravagance?

ADAM. Stop apologizing. We're building a home. White linen! It'll be a royal meal.

BEATRICE. And forgive me, but I found this pullover also. I thought it might suit you. Do you like it? You don't think it presumptuous? I'm sorry if you –

ADAM. Please, please. I can't bear you being apologetic all the time. You knew it would suit me.

BEATRICE. I'm not always sure about people, not everyone likes things bought or chosen for them.

ADAM. Not everyone likes another's choice to be so right.

(*Pause.*)

What colour shall we paint these walls?

BEATRICE. White.

ADAM. And what should be the colour of the curtains?

BEATRICE. Golden.

ADAM. And the covering for the furniture?

BEATRICE. Golden again.

ADAM. You are so sure. How quickly you answer.

BEATRICE. It's a minor accomplishment.

ADAM. Thank you. (*He moves to kiss her.*) No, I won't touch you. Won't you sit?

> (ADAM *ceremoniously pulls out a chair for her, uncorks the wine and pours their drinks. Then he takes his seat at the other end of a long table.*)

ADAM. To whom, or what, shall we drink?

BEATRICE. Perhaps we should just raise our glasses and not tempt fate.

ADAM. Are you still afraid?

BEATRICE. Afraid? I'm neither afraid nor brave. I feel nothing. Let's just drink.

> (*They raise glasses to each other and drink, slowly, remaining still when the glasses are drained.*)

BEATRICE. Do you know what my husband once said to me? 'You're like a queen', he said, 'without a country. I hate queens without their country.' He felt nothing and I felt nothing. We spent the last years living a cold courteous lie.

ADAM. But your lover?

BEATRICE. He was a leader of men.

ADAM. He was or you wanted him to be?

BEATRICE. That's just what he would have asked.

ADAM. Then I know him and I know you and I know all that passed between you.

Now you look tragic.

BEATRICE. Neither tragic nor glad. I'm indifferent.

14

(BEATRICE *fills her glass and drinks alone. They sit in silence.*
Her indifference turns to anger.)

That! That more than anything else is what I can't forgive.
He made me feel indifference. A woman like me, me –
indifference. I can't bear indifference. I despise him, the
man who dares to make me feel indifference, I despise him.

ADAM. Beatrice –

BEATRICE. From my husband I expected no more, but from
him –

ADAM. You're not talking to *me*, Beatrice.

BEATRICE. From him – to spit at the devotion I chose to give
him.

ADAM. You're not talking to *me*.

BEATRICE. He'll find no one, no one to give him so much.

ADAM. BEATRICE!

BEATRICE. No matter where he searches or for how long, no
one!

(ADAM *rises and begins clearing away.*)

BEATRICE. I'm sorry.

ADAM. I've bought some paint, we must paint the house.

BEATRICE. I'm a bore aren't I?

ADAM. From top to bottom. We must paint the house from
top to bottom if we intend to live the year out together.

BEATRICE. You're so gentle and I'm such a bore. I didn't mean
to hurt you.

ADAM. We'll greet the spring with those white walls.

BEATRICE. I don't ever mean to hurt anyone, forgive me.

ADAM. We'll greet the spring with white walls and the
summer with golden curtains.

BEATRICE. I'll look in the shops for bits and pieces, I'll make
them myself.

ADAM. What more can I do? I don't know what more I can
do. Everything explodes.

BEATRICE. I promise, I promise.

ADAM. I have a desperate need to give joy, to create laughter again, to heal someone. Isn't that obvious?

BEATRICE. I need to be healed, isn't that obvious too? I'm tired of the sound of my own voice. I need to be healed, I've destroyed a marriage and failed a lover – I need to be healed.

ADAM. You have lovely eyes, you have lovely hands.

BEATRICE. Tell me again.

ADAM. You have sweet lips.

BEATRICE. Again, again.

ADAM. And hair and skin –

BEATRICE. Tell me, Adam. Adam, tell me.

ADAM. The loud winds carry you.

BEATRICE. Heal me.

ADAM. The great gods claim you.

BEATRICE. Heal me.

ADAM. And I – I'll sit at your feet and guard you from all terror.

(*Long pause.*)

BEATRICE. And yet, you feel none of these things, do you?

ADAM. None of them.

BEATRICE. How brave are you to say them then.

ADAM. Do I need to be?

BEATRICE. I need you to be.

ADAM. I need to be.

BEATRICE. Now look at *you*. It's your face that falls apart.

ADAM. I suppose I don't really believe in the great gods.

BEATRICE. But you do. I see you do. I believe you.

ADAM. Poor Beatrice, you need to believe I do, don't you?

BEATRICE. Yes.

ADAM. And I need to be believed I suppose.

O ye gods! How we go on. We must stop this – encouraging each other's misery. Let's see how long we can stay away from morbidity. Can you use a paint brush?

BEATRICE. I can try, my lord.

ADAM. Am I your lord?

BEATRICE. You are.

ADAM. Really, really your lord?

BEATRICE. Really, really.

ADAM. Then take this brush.

(*He brings in brushes and a pail of whitewash from the kitchen; also two white aprons.*)

And wear this.

(*They dress themselves in whites, take up a brush and then turn, each a different way, looking for the wall to start on first.*)

This one?

BEATRICE. No, that one.

ADAM (*after the merest pause*). That one, then. (*They attack the wall.*)

> 'When I was a windy boy and a bit
> And the black spit of the chapel fold,
> (Sighed the old ram rod, dying of women),
> I tiptoed shy in the gooseberry wood,
> The rude owl cried like a telltale tit,
> I skipped in a blush as the big girls rolled
> Ninepin down on the donkeys' common,
> And on seesaw Sunday nights I wooed
> Whoever I would with my wicked eyes,
> The whole of the moon I could love and leave
> All the green leaved little weddings' wives
> In the coal black bush and let them grieve.
> When I was a gusty man and a half – '

BEATRICE. You recite.

ADAM.   'And the black beast of the beetles' pews – '

BEATRICE. You sing.

ADAM.   '(Sighed the old ram rod, dying of bitches),'

BEATRICE. What else do you do?

ADAM. I dance.

BEATRICE. And?

ADAM. I play the piano, the trumpet and the harp.

BEATRICE. And?

ADAM. I paint and build dams and fly space-ships.

BEATRICE. You studied engineering also then?

ADAM. And I weave tapestries.

BEATRICE. Large ones?

ADAM. Vast and intricate.

BEATRICE. Full of fantasies?

ADAM. Yes, but how did you know?

BEATRICE. How much I know about you already.

ADAM. And you?

BEATRICE. I? Oh, none of those things. Men come to me with their ideas, politicians with their doubts, poets ask my praise. My home is filled with people seeking comfort because they know my instinct is right. I know, somehow, what fits. Which woman for the right man; the correct meal for a gathering; the strength of an argument; the size of a painting for a wall. But for myself? I flutter from one grand scheme to the next and settle my mind nowhere; and yet I know that in my little finger is all the energy and the taste and the talent to shape so much, I know, so much.

ADAM. Sing, you must be able to sing.

BEATRICE. Not even that. I thought I could, till my voice rasped back at me through a tape-recorder. Somehow I can't seem to make the notes happen. A sort of moan comes out, a gurgle, a sort of gasping for air.

ADAM. Now that I find sad. That could really make me cry; that a voice can only gasp for air when it wants to sing. I don't believe you. Everybody can sing, I've never heard of anyone not being able to sing. Why it must have been the first sound of the first man.

BEATRICE. It wasn't you know. The first man gave a long wail
and ran round and round in terror. It must have been the
most nerve-racking shock in the world at that moment.
There was his wife and there were his children – and he
ran, a long, long way away. He ran.

ADAM. Wrong! It wasn't a wail of terror at all, it was a cry of
joy, a great leap in the air. And it only seemed as though
he ran a long way because he got lost in all the excitement.

BEATRICE (*through her smile*). You don't really believe that do
you, Adam?

ADAM. If I teach you to sing will you believe me?

BEATRICE. It just isn't possible, I know.

ADAM. If I give your throat a dozen notes will you believe me?

BEATRICE. You're very sweet, but –

ADAM. Will you?

BEATRICE. I –

ADAM. Will you?

> (*She is resigned.*
>
> *He hums a melodic scale.*)

Try that.

> (*A dry, awful complaint comes from her throat.*)

BEATRICE. I must be mad. Adam, believe me. I feel embarrassed.

ADAM. You didn't listen. To have produced a sound like that
you couldn't have listened.

BEATRICE. I listened, believe me, I heard you but I just
couldn't repeat it, I heard you.

ADAM. Again.

> (*Again he hums the same scale.*)

BEATRICE. Please don't make me.

ADAM. Again.

> (*He hums.*
>
> *She tries, and again a strange guttural sound comes from her
> throat.*)

But you're not listening – everybody sings.

BEATRICE. I'll cry, if you go on I'll cry.

ADAM. It's like not having eyes, or being lame. What do you do with babies if you can't lullaby them? What sound do you make when you smell the first flowers?

BEATRICE. I can't, I can't, that's it, I can't. No sound, I make no sounds, just a long moan, or a silence. I destroyed a marriage and failed a lover now leave me alone, damn you, leave me alone.

ADAM. Hush then, I'm sorry.

BEATRICE. Well I can't, I just can't sing.

ADAM. I'm sorry.

BEATRICE. I never could.

ADAM. Hush.

BEATRICE. You think I haven't tried? I've tried and I've tried, I just can't.

ADAM. I'm sorry.

My God, is there nothing we can touch that doesn't explode?

BEATRICE. Nothing.

There was nothing he or I could touch either that didn't explode.

What battles we fought. I thought I saw God in him but we fought. The boy with wings. I used to sit at his feet, literally, curled on the floor, hugging him. 'Get up,' he'd say, he hated it, 'get up, off your knees, no woman should be on her knees to a man.' He never believed he was worth such devotion, it embarrassed him.

And I was dead, a piece of nothing until he touched me, or spoke to me, or looked at me. Even his look was an embrace. I used to nag him for all his thoughts, hungry for everything that passed through his mind, jealous that he might be thinking something he couldn't share with me. And sometimes he'd be thinking of nothing and he'd say,

'Blank! My mind's a blank; must silence always signify profound thoughts, silly woman?' And I'd tell him I didn't care, I still couldn't take my eyes off him. His face was made of love, despite himself, and I knew every curve and movement his features made; I don't know why we fought.

That's a lie. I knew very well why we fought. I couldn't bear to see the shadow of another person fall on him. Even hearing him talk to someone else on the phone was enough to make prickles of the hair on my neck. How dared he think my intellect was not enough to set to right his silly world's intolerable pain! Do you know what I used to do? Oh we're awful creatures all right; sneer. I used to sneer and denigrate anyone who was near and dear to him – friends, relatives, colleagues. Even his children, lovely, large, innocent infants, even them, I couldn't bear the demands they made on him. When they were desperately ill I dismissed their complaints as childish maladies, and when they cried because their father constantly stayed away I accused them of artfulness. No one missed the whip of my sneers.

But he was a leader of men and leaders of men fight back. Every word became a sword, every sword a giant bomb destroying nerve centres, crippling the heart. We hurled anything at each other: truths, lies, half-truths – what did it matter, as long as it was poison, as long as we gave each other no peace. Sometimes he would give in, for love of me, and when the next battle came round I would taunt him with his previous surrender; and when he didn't surrender I would accuse him of being afraid of his wife. No peace, none at all, neither for him or myself.

Human communication difficult? Not for us it wasn't. We communicated only too well, he and I. In the end – we were demented, mad and demented. And for what? A love so desperate that we fought for it not to be recognized, terrified that we might reveal to each other how helpless we were. Isn't that madness? That's madness for you. Since without love I have neither appetite nor desire, I'm capable of nothing and I haven't the strength to forgive myself.

There, can you still teach me to sing? Teach me to love myself, better – then perhaps I'll sing.

(ADAM *returns to the painting.*

BEATRICE *watches him.*)

How patient you are.

(*She also takes up painting again and both continue in silence.*

Softly ADAM *begins to sing the song he sang her in winter.* BEATRICE *struggles to join him. Both are desperately trying to break her tenseness. Soon, they hum together, she slightly off-key.*

ADAM *faces us,* BEATRICE *faces* ADAM. *With slight, tentative movements she moves her hands to touch him, to reach his skin. She bares his chest.*)

Close your eyes.

(*He does so and now she unfastens her garments to bare her breasts and, gently, breast touches breast.*

Her movement is tender and sacrificial, an offering made to him for the first time; he opens his eyes and accepts it as such. Their movements are the merest and for this, the more sensual.)

ADAM. My skin breathes. There is blood flowing through my veins again. My skin breathes.

BEATRICE. Nothing should be held back, ever. I believe that, O Adam I believe that. We're mean, we're all so mean, nothing should be held back.

(*He holds her away from him to look at her face.*

She turns her face away from him.)

ADAM. You're blushing.

BEATRICE. Don't look at me.

ADAM. Like a young girl, you're blushing.

BEATRICE. Please, just hold me, don't look at me.

ADAM. Why, why? I want to look at you. Lift your head,
Beatrice, look at me. Don't turn away, look at me. Face
me, face me.

(*She falls to her knees and buries her nakedness in his limbs.*)
Wait.

(*He leaves her on her knees, clasping herself to herself, and
goes to a drawer from which he takes a shroud of golden
material. This he lays over her shoulders and raises her to her
feet.*)

There my darling. Make yourself golden clothes for the
sun. Splendid golden clothes, before the summer comes.

(BEATRICE *leaves, shrouded in a dazzling yellow cloth.*

*When she is gone he pulls back his shirt and collects
brushes and paint, calling to her as he tidies.*)

We'll paint ourselves a white temple. Do you hear that? A
white temple! I'll worship you in it. Do you hear? A white
temple to worship you in.

(*Now the scene is changed as the old walls leave and new,
white ones fly in with golden curtains in their windows; and
the old furniture is changed to a new set, of exactly the same
pieces but newly covered in the same golden material. When
this is done he surveys his work and leaves, satisfied.*

The days have passed, the weeks, even.)

Part Two

SUMMER

BEATRICE *enters.*

It is a new morning and, beautifully dressed in a yellow garment of the material she left in, she approaches the room, the day, the sun as though for the first time.

She is in love with the room, the morning and herself. She stands before a mirror and stretches her limbs long and sensuously; then, embarrassed, she turns away and giggles to herself. In this mood she wanders round the room touching its many textures, realizing them perhaps for the first time.

ADAM *enters and watches her for some seconds before she turns to him. They approach each other and now, not for the first time, but remembering, she feels the shape of his body.*

He is about to speak but she gestures him not to. She does not want to talk, only to look at him, and this she does with a sort of incredulity, as though she cannot believe her good fortune. She pulls him gently round the room in order to see him in different lights. At times she moves a long way away from him and wanders round the room, at a great distance, as though to approach him would make him disappear. Every so often she turns her back on him and then turns swiftly back as though imagining he might be gone, as though tempting fate to take him.

When they are at such a distance, suddenly, the furniture and the walls of the room fly away. The 'tree' is there; the sun is yellow; they are out in the fields.

BEATRICE, *like a young girl, tucks her dress into her pants while* ADAM *bends to touch his toes and she, with a great 'whoop', runs and leaps over his back. Then he leaps over her.*

Now they just walk and walk, breathing the air, touching their finger tips, each stretching, each feeling the shape of their own bodies.

BEATRICE. There is blood flowing through my veins again. My skin breathes.

(*Soon they lie down, by a bank, under a tree, near a rick.*)

ADAM. Look at that bird, that one there, the one that just seems to be hanging in the air – do you believe it?

BEATRICE. Believe it?

ADAM. Believe in it.

BEATRICE. In its existence?

ADAM. No, no. Not its existence; I mean, well look at it. You can't really believe that it can stay in the air, just by flapping about like that, can you? Or can you? I suppose you can.

BEATRICE. What keeps it in the air then?

ADAM. Oh, I don't know. Someone under the ground keeps blowing up I suppose; I can't think of any other reason. Like aeroplanes, all that metal in the air. All that metal and all those people, stuck in the air, with nothing underneath them.

BEATRICE. Except air.

ADAM. Except air.

BEATRICE. Blown by somebody under the earth.

ADAM. And ships. Silly isn't it? That mass of iron and wood –

BEATRICE. – and people –

ADAM. – and people, all floating –

BEATRICE. – with nothing underneath them –

ADAM. – except frogmen. Thousands of them. Swimming with one arm and holding up the boat with the other.

BEATRICE. And clouds.

ADAM. Clouds?

BEATRICE. Making all that noise, thunder – at least so they say.

ADAM. Oh that one. I've never believed that one.

BEATRICE. I mean what's a cloud? Mist! Nothing!

ADAM. And those flowers.

BEATRICE. Which ones?

ADAM. Those, over there, with all those colours and patterns –
you know what they say about those don't you?

BEATRICE. What?

ADAM. That they – you won't believe this – that they come
from a tiny seed, no bigger than this. All those colours,
look! No bigger than this.

BEATRICE. They tried to tell me that one at school.

ADAM. Did you believe them?

BEATRICE. I planted forests, once, in a remote part of the
Highlands, for two years, reclaiming lost land. My father
studied plants and I learned from him the drama of watching things grow. And when my university days were over
I took to the hills and bandaged dying firs and damaged
pines.

Have you ever heard of the *Soldanella* or the Shasta
Daisy? The White *Lauristinus* and the Red Ice Plant? Did
you know that *Convalaria majalis* was the Latin name for
lily of the valley? 'Consider the *Convalaria majalis* how they
grow, they toil not, neither do they spin: and yet I say
unto you that even Solomon in all his glory was not
arrayed like one of these.'

I made things grow, Adam, once I made things grow.

ADAM. And now?

BEATRICE. Now? I have a golden eagle for a lover.

ADAM. But the sun has burnt his wings.

BEATRICE. Nothing shall burn your wings – I am your sun.

ADAM. Where shall I fly?

BEATRICE. Anywhere – as long as you carry me with you.

ADAM. But you're my sun.

BEATRICE. When you need me to be your sun, I'm your sun.
When you need soft winds I shall cover the land with my
breath. When you need comfort then I shall offer my

breasts and my limbs and my lips. Whatever you call for you shall have.

ADAM. And you? What shall I give you?

BEATRICE. Every second. Every touch, every thought, every feeling. Every second you shall give me.

ADAM. 'Shall'? You demand?

BEATRICE. Do you deny me the right to demand?

ADAM. I deny you nothing.

BEATRICE (leaping up). I HAVE A GOLDEN EAGLE FOR A LOVER! A GOLDEN EAGLE! I HAVE A GOLDEN EAGLE FOR A LOVER! Adam, are we ready? Are we ready now? Let's go now. Let's test ourselves away from here. Before the winter comes let's go away from this house, now, now. This is the loveliest time, let's go –

ADAM. Now?

BEATRICE. Now, now! If we stay on we'll tempt fate.

ADAM. Not yet. Trust me.

BEATRICE. Don't you see what's happened to me? Dear God! I believe in everything. I would like to be young again for you; I would like to be shy and pure and untouched for you. Let's go, Adam. We've had this place, this time – we've had it, all it can give. There's nothing more here. Let's go.

ADAM. Trust me.

BEATRICE. Trust you? Oh I trust everything to you. I could tear myself apart for you, I could fly for you. I'm a flower, Adam see me? See me opening, watch me, I'm blossoming, watch me, watch meeeeee.

(BEATRICE *towers and slowly stretches out to the sun. The movement of her body matches the words she cries.*

She faces the sun.

ADAM *watches her turn to the sun and place her back to him.*

He turns and moves away from her.

They freeze in this position.
The sun sets.
The walls and furniture return.
The days are passing, the weeks, even.)

ADAM. There are two kinds of love and there are two kinds of women. The woman whose love is around you, keeping its distance lest the heat of it burns you; and out of that warmth you emerge, slowly, confidently, as sure as the seed in her womb. And the woman whose love is an oppressive sun burning the air around you till you can't breath and drying every drop of moisture from your lips till you can't speak; and she has a passion no part of which relates to any living man nor any living man could share.

You know, when I was born I was born with a great laughter in me. Can you believe that? A great laughter, like a blessing. And some people loved and some hated it. It was a sort of challenge, a test against which people measured themselves as human beings; and I could never understand, not at all, the desperateness of either their love or their hatred. Have you ever been with a beautiful woman, a really breathtaking beauty, and watched or felt the passionate waves of devotion and loathing that she attracts, and noticed how the people around feel the irresistible need to say sly, unpleasant things to show they're not intimidated by her beauty? So it was with my laughter.

And she, who had no need to measure herself against anything or anyone because she was so endowed with her own loveliness, her own intelligence – she too began to measure herself against that laughter. And why? Because it belonged to me you see; I was *born* with it, she couldn't bear that it had not been bestowed by her and so she began to measure herself against me and challenge all that was mine.

She found enemies where there were none and saw betrayals in every act. She broke each smile and stormed every moment of peace we had built. And once, when I wrote to her from a sick bed and cursed her, when I lost control, she suddenly became calm and took control as if to show that in fact she had bestowed that laughter on me, and only she could nurse me back to health. 'That laughter is our child,' she said. 'Now, at last, only I can look after it. You', she said 'are incapable.'

Soon, there was no sense to her words. 'I see God in you,' she used to say, and then she poured sourness on my work. She would thank me for giving her life and then boast how she had made me. She would rave and regret, applaud and destroy, love and devour. Mad, mad mad mad woman.

Why does a woman destroy her love with such a desperate possessiveness, why? She had no need to be desperate – I was possessed.

Where is she now, I wonder? God knows! Contemplating the ruins she made, I suppose; startled, surprised at the emptiness around her after all the violence of those times. Dazed with the bits and pieces of life she's left with. 'How did it happen?' she's saying. 'What was I doing?' Lonely, unutterably lonely.

Dear God, she deserves her loneliness. No one has the right to take away laughter from a man, or deny a woman her beauty. She deserves her misery. And yet, despite what she is, there is a part of her that does not deserve what she is; I always understood.

Through all that madness – and it is a madness you know, love like that, a madness – but through it all I understood her need to howl at the pain of such a tortuous relationship. And she understood, also. In moments of peace we both understood and comforted each other. But then she would forget and she would howl again and I could never forgive her that her howl carried such terror, that her wounds spilt not clear blood but a venomous poison and that it went on and on and on and on, relentlessly, crippling us both. Dear God, she deserves her loneliness.

And I? I rummage about the world looking for bits and pieces of old passions, past enthusiasms and echoes of old laughter. But it's a feeble search, really. I see things wanting her to see them. I visit places wanting her to be with me. I think thoughts wanting her to share them, crying out for her praise. All that I do from the drinks I drink to the gardens I grow, from the colours I adore to the moods I make – all, everything is the pale reflection of her vivid personality.

We never recover, do we? With her the laughter turned into cries of pain; without her the laughter is gone. We never really recover.

(*When* BEATRICE *turns to him she is a changed woman. The venom of her words is matched by the hardness in her eyes.*)

BEATRICE. You dare tell me all this?

ADAM. Dare? I confide in you. Why 'dare'?

BEATRICE. Not one thought should you be thinking that is not directed at me.

ADAM. Beatrice!

BEATRICE. At me! Not one thought.

ADAM. But I'm trusting you. With confidences, I'm trusting you.

BEATRICE. And I trusted you. With my love.

ADAM. You've not understood.

BEATRICE. You, my 'golden eagle'.

ADAM. You can't have been listening.

BEATRICE. My husband always used to say to me I expected too much from people.

ADAM. I've exposed myself – you can't have been listening.

BEATRICE. To make me witness to such insensitivity.

ADAM. Insensitivity? That, you call insensitivity?

BEATRICE. Such crudeness.

ADAM. Did you want passionate lies?

BEATRICE. Passionate lies?

ADAM. Mean pretences?

BEATRICE. Mean pretences? Is that what our time has been? Your singing, your poetry recitals, your declarations from the clouds? Mean pretence?

ADAM. These are familiar battlegrounds, Beatrice; don't let's pursue them.

BEATRICE. Why not? Are you afraid of what might be said? My brave hero? Sent by the gods to protect me?

ADAM. Let's be wise, recognize the warning. We're tired, don't pursue these familiar battlegrounds.

(ADAM *retreats from her by taking out an easel and canvas upon which he starts to paint.*)

BEATRICE. Familiar for us both.

ADAM. For us both then. And so you should understand. Be generous and understand. I listened to your laments, now be generous, listen to my fears. Look at you, you're shaking with rage, you're not even listening.

BEATRICE. I hear every word.

ADAM. You hear what you want to hear, you understand what you need to understand.

BEATRICE. You see things wanting her to see them, you think thoughts wanting her to share them – fight me.

ADAM. You're right.

BEATRICE. Fight me.

ADAM. I've made a mistake.

34

BEATRICE. Fight me.

ADAM. I was insensitive. I'm sorry. Now, let this day pass.

BEATRICE. Oh no! Not like that you don't dismiss me. I have a right to be answered, I've given you my love, I have a right to be consoled.

ADAM. Rights? Rights? We now demand rights.

BEATRICE. You're afraid.

ADAM. A growing tree blots out the sun.

BEATRICE. I raised my arms to the sun and you were afraid.

ADAM. Yes, afraid. And look how you know it.

BEATRICE. I grow and you become terrified.

ADAM. Yes, yes, terrified; and stop pretending all that innocence.

BEATRICE. You poor thing you.

ADAM. Every time a woman raises her arms to the sun for the man she wants a great battle-cry goes up and the war goes on.

BEATRICE. You poor, pathetic thing, you.

ADAM. And I try to believe it can't be true, not all the time, but it is. It goes on and on.

BEATRICE. There is neither fight nor love in you.

(Pause.)

ADAM. No love in me? You think that? I'll not fight you, Beatrice. I'm neither pathetic nor afraid, just weary.

(Long pause.)

BEATRICE. Why do you paint? A professor of words why do you dabble on canvas? You're not very good at it.

ADAM. Oh your sneering is too accomplished for me.

BEATRICE. I'm not sneering, you just can't paint. Why this need for hobbies? Don't your students adore you enough? The great authority on the Romantic poets? Why this need for week-end pastimes?

ADAM. I'm weary, Beatrice, weary and sick.

BEATRICE. Sick?

ADAM. My body feels like crumbling.

35

BEATRICE. Psychosomatic. You look perfectly healthy to me. You can't avoid me by retreating into illness.

ADAM. How could I, how could I have made the same mistake again?

BEATRICE. Poor Adam.

ADAM. You don't say 'poor Beatrice'?

BEATRICE. Why should I?

ADAM. No, indeed, why should you.

> (*They are not facing each other.*
>
> *There is a long silence.*)

BEATRICE. Adam? I'm cold.

ADAM. The leaves are falling, there's a heavy wind.

BEATRICE. I need something to keep me warm. (*Silence.*) No suggestions these days? Your lady is cold, is there no longer a guard to attend her? (*Silence.*) And your silence is even colder. Adam, your poor lady is cold.

ADAM. I have these.

> (*From a drawer he takes out two pullovers. One is brown, the other is rust.*
>
> *The brown one he puts on himself, the other he pulls down over* BEATRICE.
>
> *They are now dressed in autumnal colours, green, golden, brown and rust.*)

BEATRICE. Why don't *you* warm me?

> (*He needs to, fears to, but finally takes her in his arms.*
>
> ADAM *kisses her, it is a long, long kiss.*
>
> *The light changes.*
>
> *The days pass, the weeks, even.*)

> (*Suddenly* ADAM *falls limp in her arms.*)

BEATRICE. Adam! Oh, it's games now is it? Adam!

Really, it's very boyish and charming but I'm a mature

woman, games irritate me. (*She waits.*) Adam, don't weary me, please.

(*She lowers him to the divan and moves away to attend to the room.*)

Adam, I know you want to cheer me up but I'm afraid that some of the games you play are not right for the age we have. Adam! Adam!

(*Now she moves to him and turns him over.*)

My God how white your face has turned. ADAM!

(*She places her hand on his forehead.*)

But there was no sign. What have you caught you foolish boy? There was no sign. Such a fever – foolish boy such a fever.

(*She lays a blanket over him and then pulls a small table and armchair to the bedside. From a sideboard she withdraws a bottle of brandy and a glass which she places to* ADAM's lips.

When he has drunk some she kisses him.

During her next words the light again changes as she spends the next weeks looking after him.)

Now you are so precious, so precious to me. I would die tending you.

(ADAM *moves and murmurs.*)

I'm here my lovely one, right here. No need to cry out. Hush. Lie still, I'm here, feel me.

(*Now she places a blanket around her shoulders and sits by his side to await his recovery.*)

How I wish I could sing now. You're right, it is a kind of crippling when your voice can't make music. You know, I'm not really as treacherous as I sound, or cold or humourless. Sometimes a fever gets in me too and I don't know what I say. But I'm always honest, at least to myself, and good and really – very wise.

37

But I'm damaged, I blush for the creases in my skin, I'm ashamed of my worn limbs, second-hand. Third-hand to be precise; third-hand bruised and damaged – like a clock striking midnight when the hour is only six, and it wheezes and whirrs. But the hands always point to the right time. And if we had met each other before we had met anyone else then the hands would have pointed to the right time and the right hour would have sung clear and ringing.

Oh, if we had met before we'd been touched by anyone else, you and I. You, Adam, and I – what would we have done together? What wouldn't we have done together! Burned paths of sweet-smelling flowers across the world, and gone looking in all its curious corners, raised storms among the dead – that's what we'd have done. Do you know what my husband once said to me? 'You're like a queen', he said, 'without her country. I hate queens', he said, 'without their countries.'

And he was right. A queen without a country or a king. No home and no man to pay me homage. All my life I have looked for peace and majesty, for a man who was unafraid and generous; generous and not petty. I can't bear little men; mean, apologetic, timid men; men who mock themselves and sneer at others; who delight in downfall and dare nothing. Peace, majesty and great courage – how I've longed for those things.

He once abandoned me in a fog, that man, that man I called God; in a long, London fog, left me, to walk home alone.

Peace, majesty and great courage.

And once I ran through a storm of rain and stood on a station platform, soaking and full of tears, pleading with him to take me, take me, take me with him. And he wanted to take me, I know it, but he refused to show his need. Through an afternoon of rain, I ran.

Sometimes he took me with him and we'd walk through streets of strange towns discovering new shapes to the houses and breathing new airs.

Peace, majesty and great courage – never. I've found none of these things. Such bitter disappointment. Bitter. Bitter, bitter, bitter. And out of such bitterness cruelty grows. You cannot understand the cruelty that grows. And I meant none of it, not one cruel word of it. And he knew and I knew and we both knew that we knew, yet the cruelty went on.

But laments for what's done and past are not a way to cure an invalid are they? I should be making plans for to-morrow shouldn't I? For when you get up, and the day after, and the month after and all those long years we'll have together. What shall we do in those years, Adam? Eh? All those great long years ahead? Shall we set to right the silly world's intolerable pains? I have plans, of children and travel and daring all those things you didn't dare be-fore. And you have plans. We'll plot and build each moment like schemers of a great ball where all the guests shall come to pay homage and share the joy of those two brilliant lovers. And peace, above all – peace, and trust and majesty and all that great courage.

Get well my darling boy and you'll see. My voice may not sing but my love does. Get well.

(ADAM *sits up* .)

ADAM. How long has it been?

BEATRICE. The weeks have passed.

ADAM. And have you stayed with me that long?

BEATRICE. Hush.

ADAM. Weeks? And you've stayed by me all that time?

BEATRICE. Yes. But don't imagine it was an effort because it wasn't. It sounds more heroic than it was, I suffer from insomnia, it came easily.

39

ADAM. What a strange fever it was. I've never been so ill before.

BEATRICE. Fatigue, tension, quite common really.

ADAM. Are you trying to take the drama out of it? I feel very weak and sad – I'm enjoying it. With you at my side, tenderness all about you. You're like a woman who's just given birth – all glowing and slightly smug. I'm being spoilt and cared for, it's nice, I'm enjoying it.

(ADAM *now rises from his sick bed, his blanket over his shoulder, and moves to look out of the window.*)

The days get shorter. You can smell days getting shorter can't you?

(*He moves to look at the canvas he's been dabbling on.*)

You're right of course. I dabble. I should be content with words, even though they're other people's words.

BEATRICE. 'Despise not the teacher for from him comes a love the most unselfish of all.'

ADAM. If only you were as gentle and generous as that always.

BEATRICE. Aren't I?

No, I'm not. Perhaps because I dabble also. How else do we know how to sneer at others if not because we've sneered at ourselves so well? I dabble and so I recognize the dabbler, the dilettante.

You don't contradict me? That's not very gallant.

ADAM. You have an original mind. You know what I think. You don't need me for flattery.

BEATRICE. How wrong you are. To believe in the nonsense of honesty, how wrong you are. Most women need the warmth of men's lies. Do you think it satisfies me to hear you say I have an original mind? I know that. But my deficiences, my failings, these need sustenance. Employ your encouragement there. Reassure me, that one day I'll do what doesn't bore me, that I won't always despise the people who rush to me for advice.

ADAM. Was I sick? My stomach feels so empty, I feel so thin. And you stayed through the smell and ugliness of all that? We've known each other a long time now haven't we?

(*Both in their separate places let the blankets drop from their shoulders. The days pass, the weeks, even.*)

(*The preparations for the strudel.*)

ADAM. It's a long time since I've made one. Two things my grandmother bequeathed me in her will, a bag full of mint farthings and the recipe for Hungarian apple strudel.

(*He is looking for white aprons.*)

Here, you'll also need to wear one. The dust flies, I warn you.

(*He wrings his hands, like a pianist before the concert, exaggerating the movements.*)

You know, my son used to say that the colour of the wind was black.

BEATRICE. That's depressing.

ADAM. No, it's positive. Black! He was certain of it, couldn't be any other colour. Black! And he even used to smile as though I must be teasing to ask a question with such an obvious answer.

BEATRICE. What colour do you think it is?

ADAM. Grey. The wind is grey.

And now, the miracle.

BEATRICE. The miracle! I've been waiting so long for this miracle.

ADAM. It's magical, I promise you. Everything prepared?

BEATRICE. As you asked for. Sliced apples, cleaned nuts.

ADAM. The rest?

BEATRICE. Raisins, caster sugar, cinnamon and olive oil.

(BEATRICE *brings these items out on to the sideboard.*

ADAM *is about to make apple strudel;[1] the process is a very dramatic one.*

The paste has been 'resting' for twenty minutes. He is about to collect it from the kitchen. But first he throws a table-cloth over the table. The magician prepares!

Now he retrieves the paste from the kitchen; it is lying on a plate, covered by a floured cloth. The paste sits like a round loaf. He picks it from the plate, gingerly since it flops about, though it should come away clean if the plate has been well floured, and he is about to lay it on the centre of the table.)

ADAM. The flour!

In the kitchen, quick, I took it there to dust this plate. For God's sake, the paste is drooping, quick.

(BEATRICE *hastens to find the flour and returns to dust, sprinkle, strew the table-cloth with it.*

ADAM *lays his paste in the centre of the cloth, reaches for a rolling pin, dusts that with flour, and rolls it out to the first oval stage.*)

ADAM. Pretty?

(BEATRICE *shrugs her shoulders.*)

You're a hard woman, Beatrice.

BEATRICE. Hard? How short-sighted you are. I'm soft, like this dough, only a bit tastier.

ADAM. You've made a joke. You didn't mean to but you made a joke. It's the first time.

BEATRICE. Your paste, attend to your paste.

ADAM. Hard. Not a bit of praise. Mean.

BEATRICE. When you've earned your praise I'll give it, lavishly. Your paste.

ADAM. Oil, hot oil, in the kitchen.

(*He holds out his hand like a doctor calling for the scalpel, never taking his eyes off the paste.*

[1] Culinary notes are at the end of the play.

42

A sceptical BEATRICE *moves slowly off.*)

Move, woman. Quick.

(ADAM *is delighted and walks round and round his paste.*)

BEATRICE. 'Quick!' he cries.

(*But she does move faster and brings* ADAM *his oil. He pours a thimbleful over the paste and then spreads it over the surface with his palm.*)

ADAM. Ouch! It's hot. Now (*to himself*) make sure it covers the surface, help it stretch, gently, and – wait.

Now, you just sit there and – watch.

(*He looks triumphantly at* BEATRICE *who again shrugs her shoulders.*)

Hard, so hard.

BEATRICE. You find delight in such small things.

ADAM. Small things? Small things? You've seen nothing, nothing yet. The miracle begins now.

(*And sure enough, the miracle does begin now, for* ADAM *begins to stretch his paste and does so to the accompaniment of much gentle clowning; gentle, gentle, not frantic, clowning.*)

Pull my beauty, pull, pull. Stay moist, don't harden yet, stay moist.

(BEATRICE *impatiently rises and turns her attention to the room.*)

Why do you keep emptying ashtrays and tidying up? Keep still and watch me.

BEATRICE. Dirt offends me.

ADAM. You can't cope with disorder can you?

BEATRICE. Yes, I can cope with disorder, only dirty and ugly things I can't bear.

ADAM. You're so fussy.

BEATRICE. No. Fussiness belongs to pedants. I'm not a pedant, just right!

(*He brings her back to the chair to ensure she is watching before resuming his work.*)

43

ADAM. A hole! Damn, a hole! Lack of practice. Still, not a big one. Must keep my eye on that, have to patch it if it grows.

BEATRICE. I'm sure the clowning and gestures are not essential.

ADAM. Cruel. You're cruel and hard. Here, drink some milk, soften yourself.

BEATRICE. I can't bear milk. It's for women who throw javelins. I prefer lemons.

ADAM. Sour. Sour and hard. Your eyes should be growing wider and wider, you should be astonished at my skill.

BEATRICE. I confess – it's fascinating.

ADAM. How begrudgingly you say it. Damn, another hole. Small, it's small though. Wha hoo! Wha hoo!

(ADAM *has reached the stage where he can flap the pastry, like a sheet on a bed, to straighten it out.*)

Isn't that a marvellous sight?

BEATRICE. Very clever, yes.

ADAM. Why – you're irritated.

BEATRICE. Am I?

ADAM. Why are you irritated?

BEATRICE. Look, another hole, attend to your holes.

ADAM. Why are you irritated?

BEATRICE. I'm sorry, I can't share your miracle.

ADAM. Of course you can. Learn, you can learn can't you? Tomorrow you'll make one. You're jealous aren't you?

BEATRICE. Jealous!

ADAM. Ha ha! She's jealous. Pull, my beauty, pull, pull. Did I ever tell you about my student days? About the time I nearly set fire to the kitchen I worked in? I dipped a panier of wet chips into boiling hot fat. Don't laugh. I thought the wet chips would cool the fat down; no one ever told me that when you put water to hot fat it ignites.

BEATRICE. What happened?

ADAM. It ignited. I just stood there, watching the flames,

44

mesmerized. And the chefs and maintenance men ran backwards and forwards screaming and trying to smother the flames with some sticky stuff and I just stood there, watching. Of course I was paralysed with surprise so I stood still, and everyone thought I was being calm. I ended the hero.

There, it's done. And only a few holes. Now apples. (*He strews apples along the edge of the table.*)

Cinnamon. (*He dusts with cinnamon.*) Nuts. (*He strews the nuts.*) Raisins. (*He scatters the raisins.*) Sugar. (*He attends to the sugar.*) More cinnamon. (ADAM *sprinkles another coat of cinnamon.*) Clean up (*and takes a knife and cuts away the thick edges of paste hanging all round the table*). Now we roll.

(ADAM *clutches each end of the table-cloth under the hanging paste and gently rolls and encloses the contents of the strudel into a long pipe. When it's done he hastily drips more olive oil over the surface of the long strudel, sprinkles more sugar into the oil, cuts it into three lengths, lays the three lengths on to an oven tray and, swiftly, pushes all into the oven, snapping the door shut in triumph.*)

ADAM. Now, tell me, why were you so irritated?

BEATRICE. You were so absorbed.

ADAM. But I did it for you. For you to watch, for you to learn, for you to eat.

BEATRICE. That's how it started, perhaps. But half way through I –

ADAM. What? Half way through you – ?

BEATRICE. I'm ashamed.

ADAM. Half way through you – ?

BEATRICE. I'm so stupid and ashamed.

ADAM. You – ?

BEATRICE. I became afraid.

ADAM. Afraid?

BEATRICE. Oh don't go on. If you can't understand don't go on.

ADAM. You can't dismiss me like that – I want to understand.

BEATRICE. I shouldn't need to tell you.

ADAM. All right, I'm a fool. Tell me.

BEATRICE. You just want me to say it don't you?

ADAM. Yes.

BEATRICE. You do understand, don't you?

ADAM. Yes.

BEATRICE. It's your laughter. I can't bear your laughter, it's unnatural. It casts everybody out.

ADAM. Everybody?

BEATRICE. Well me, then.

ADAM. You resent my laughter?

BEATRICE. Every second. Every touch, every thought, every feeling, every second you should give to me.

ADAM. And then there would come a moment when every touch would be flinched from, every thought would be sneered at and every feeling abused.

BEATRICE. And that's the moment you're afraid of?

ADAM. Yes.

BEATRICE. You think me capable of abuse?

ADAM. All women.

BEATRICE. But me? Me? Capable of abuse?

ADAM. All women.

BEATRICE. I see.

> (*The tidying is done.*
> *They move apart.*
> *The days are passing, the weeks, even.*)

AUTUMN

The walls and the furniture move. They stand, each alone, looking at the sky; a wind blows.

The light changes from dusk to night. It is a brilliantly clear, brisk night, full of stars.

BEATRICE. What are you thinking?

ADAM. If I said my mind's a blank, would you believe me?

BEATRICE. If you say so.

> (*Pause.*)
>
> Is it?
>
> (*Pause.*)
>
> Do those stars inspire only blankness?
>
> (*Pause.*)
>
> Why didn't you love your wife?

ADAM. Why didn't you love your husband?

BEATRICE. Why? There are no reasons. One day you just look at somebody and realize that you don't love them. No hate, no anger –

ADAM. Just guilt for being unable to feel what is expected and needed from you.

BEATRICE. But guilt needs a reason doesn't it, Adam?

ADAM. And so you begin looking for the reasons; and you find that all those things that before just irritated you, nothing more, just irritated you, you begin magnifying into massive excuses for hate. You know, I can't think of anything I've done that I haven't felt guilty for.

The first girl I ever loved was when I was twelve years old. She had a pink face and a cheeky smile and she thought she was ugly. I couldn't persuade her that she wasn't. She pouted her lips and protected herself behind large, wise round eyes as if she knew before love came that love was an impossible dream. For four years I wooed her until, at last, a moment came when she finally trusted herself in my arms; and in that moment, that very same moment, I betrayed her.

It happened at a camp in a valley, near one of the largest forests I'd ever seen. We went each summer, for four years, just a group of us.

And on the last summer there came a girl who took one look at me and decided – what were her own words now? She told me afterwards – she had decided, from the start, to 'net me'. Net me! What a woman in the making she was. Tongue like a whip. Will, like a great boulder; and intelligence, sharp, like a frightened hawk. And I was to carry her scars for ever. Because while I wooed my child-hood sweetheart this miniature adult weaved her own and subtle net with a terrible, terrible precision. And on the last night she, my wide-eyed sweetheart, and I, at last, after four years, managed, somehow, to find that sort of exhaustion which earned us the trust of each other's arms. I'd won. There we lay, among friends and the smell of wet canvas – she wasn't really in my arms but on them, and I think I kissed her cheek, once, or perhaps twice, nothing more, and then she fell asleep. And as she was lying on my arm, another hand reached out for me, and – I took it.

I lie here, under these stars, and I think about camp and I remember that camp and I know, as sure as I know that there's a cloud on that moon, that for that one terrible act of betrayal I have paid and wrecked my once and only life with every act and decision I've ever made. That's what I'm thinking.

Do you know, a friend and I once ran all the way across three fields and up a hill to see a sun set? Without stopping, all the way, imagine that – I ran, like a lunatic, to catch a sun setting in some Cotswold hill.

How difficult it is to believe we were ever once happy. (*Long pause.*)

BEATRICE. Silent now? Are you silent now? Poor Adam, how I know that need to be silent. Won't you tell me what I can do? Won't you even say two words? Like 'touch me' or 'kiss me' or 'go away' even? But I don't want to go away. I can't bear your misery. Suddenly I want to take you in my arms and give you such comfort. Suddenly I want to protect you. What can I do? Won't you give me a command, like you used to? Command me. I'm your mistress – don't you know you can use me as you like? Don't you know you have that power?

You haven't the strength to use me, have you? Nor the will, not the slightest will in the world.

Perhaps there's somewhere I can take you. Perhaps we should find another house; the country must be full of deserted houses. Wouldn't that be strange? We could spend the rest of our lives going from house to house, re-decorating each of them, and in the one I could revive you till all my energy was spent and in the next you would revive me and so we'd go on.

But we never really recover, do we? Not really.

Do you know what day it is – I almost forgot – don't you remember? It's Guy Fawkes day. We bought some fireworks. You'd forgotten hadn't you? Fireworks, Adam.

(*She looks round, anxious to find something to re-engage his spirits. She spies the 'tree', runs to it and brings it to the centre stage. Then she takes out the branches and sticks them through some holes in the drainpipe to form the arms of a 'guy'.*

ADAM, *depressed, can barely respond, and simply moves into*

*the house to return with a jacket, scarf and hat. They both
dress the 'guy'.)*

BEATRICE. Shall I set them up?

ADAM. No, I'll set them up. You stay here, look at the moon
or count the stars, you stay here.

(BEATRICE *watches him move despondently away. There is
no more they can do for each other. She turns to the guy,
which she now sees as a scarecrow.)*

BEATRICE. Babies, corpses, scarecrows – *you* can't respond
either, can you? I can talk to you, blossom for you and
tear myself apart, but it would be the same. The straw in
you would burn and burn and then – nothing. Dead
cinders of nothing, nothing, nothing. Peace, majesty and
great courage? Dear God – you made them images of
limp cloth, not clay, and gave us a passion to be spent on
air, cold night air.

(*The first firework explodes. A distant boom, a soft echo of
light – like approaching battle.*

ADAM *returns.*)

ADAM. Boom! They're off. Like fireworks, do you? Boom!
There goes the second one. My children did. Boom!
Pretty, aren't they? Allow me to show you a photograph
of one of my children. Do you know I've never shown a
photograph of my children to anyone before? Would you
believe that? You won't be embarrassed by photographs,
will you? Here, look at that grin. Look at the way his arms
fold. Defiant! That's him. Stubborn and defiant, in charge.
A king of a kingdom of infants and that kingdom is all
toy trains and problems.

(ADAM *strikes the pose of the child in the photograph.*

*The fireworks continue in intermittent distant booms and
glows of light.*)

BEATRICE. Yes, he looks like you. What is it pasted to? A
Christmas card? Of your son?

ADAM. It's a Christmas card of a child.

BEATRICE. He actually sent a Christmas card with a photo-graph of his son on it. What bad taste. I blush for you.

ADAM. I sent it because it's a good photograph of a child, not because it's my son.

BEATRICE. Like a politician endearing himself to the public. You have children like possessions don't you? Did you show it to your mistress? Every time you made love? Did you? Take it out and sigh over it, to show how guilty you felt? Did you talk about your wife in bed? Say how good she really was? Did you? Did you tell your other mistress the story of the girl at camp? Did you? Did you? DID YOU?

ADAM. You're possessed aren't you? Something moves in you that you can't control doesn't it? Can't you hear yourself? Don't you ever hear yourself? Don't you ever feel ashamed? The same, always the same lamentations, lamentably always the same. All my life I have looked for a woman who had that touch of magic. Whose words would not be dragged out of that decrepit old box of hag's tricks.

BEATRICE. A Christmas card of your son!

ADAM. You've not even heard. Not one word have you heard. You can neither hear nor understand that you're not hearing.

BEATRICE. I think I see you now. Go home to your wife. She'll forgive you. There's nothing more you can do here.

ADAM. You've never even dared to have a child, have you?

BEATRICE. No man with any sensitivity would have said that.

ADAM. You make up the rules as you go along.

BEATRICE. My 'golden eagle'. His son on a Christmas card.

ADAM. How treacherous, crude, destructive you are.

BEATRICE. Oh call me the names you want. I'm indifferent to your scorn.

51

ADAM. It was not love you needed was it? Was it? I don't think you're capable of love are you? Eh? Capable of it? Are you capable of real love?

BEATRICE. Yes.

ADAM. Really capable?

BEATRICE. Yes, yes.

ADAM. Are you?

BEATRICE. Yes, yes. Love. Real love. I – CAN – LOVE.

ADAM. How loudly you need to say it.

BEATRICE. I – can – love. I – have – loved. Always. And look what comes back – the smell of guilt, the pathetic smell of guilt. I – can – love. Not you though. Look at you. Rigid with terror, fear, stiff with fear. Tight with it. Tight. Tight, tight, tight.

ADAM. The sounds you make, I know you make the sounds, the sounds and the gestures of love. But feelings? Nothing.

BEATRICE. My dear, you're not the best person to talk about feelings are you? Not exactly the best, the most faithful. Ah those nights at camp with – what was it? – the smell of wet canvas?

ADAM. Nothing, nothing can be trusted with you.

BEATRICE. Don't imagine you confided things to me that I couldn't already see. Or did you think I was ever really taken in by your waxwork passion?

ADAM. I gave you what was precious to me. What you needed I gave you and it was precious to me.

BEATRICE. You? You were never big enough to give me what I needed. But I'll survive.

ADAM. Won't you, just.

BEATRICE. You won't. They won't and you won't but I've more guts and passion than the three of you together. I'll survive.

ADAM. You sound like *her*. She was so insistent on her ability

to survive that the last time I went to see her she played a
record of Beethoven's fifth symphony.

BEATRICE. Ha! Even to the end you're cruel. You feel
nothing.

ADAM. I'm too shocked to feel.

BEATRICE. I warned you. I asked you to come away from this
place didn't I?

ADAM. That's the reason is it?

BEATRICE. I warned you. You were not big enough.

ADAM. That's the reason.

BEATRICE. Now go home.

ADAM. I didn't fly off with you.

BEATRICE. You couldn't keep one mistress, give this one up.
Go home.

ADAM. You couldn't wait to bring back the spoils.

BEATRICE (*mocking*). You see things wanting her to see them,
you think thoughts wanting her to share them – go home.

ADAM. You failed two men and now you need to show that it
wasn't your fault.

BEATRICE. Who can't be trusted with confessions, who?

ADAM. Oh, you're righteous about betrayal now are you?

BEATRICE. You little piece of man, you. You dare throw back
at me what I confided in you?

ADAM. You drag dirt from me.

BEATRICE. Go home to your comforts.

ADAM. You oppress me.

BEATRICE. To your wife, go home.

ADAM. You dry up the air around me.

BEATRICE. To your grinning brats – go, go.

(ADAM *slaps her face.*)

You dare lift your hands to me? You dare?

(*She raises her hands to attack him but he holds her wrists.*)

ADAM. Nothing touches you. You devour, devour, devour,
DEVOUR!

(*He releases her.*)

BEATRICE. I despise you. Go home.

(*The walls return, the furniture also.*
The days pass, the weeks, even.)

(ADAM *is now left confronting the scarecrow.* BEATRICE *creeps to a corner of the room, retreating once more into misery and tears.*)

ADAM. Babies, corpses, scarecrows – you don't answer back do you? I confess my fears and you have such a silence, such a reassuring silence. You'll take me as I am won't you? We all know ourselves don't we? Who needs to be told? Good old boy. The only thing is, when I give you my love you don't return it, and that's the hell of it. Only a human being can return that and the price you pay is the advantage they take. That's the hell of it.

BEATRICE. I saw God in you.

ADAM. You saw in me what you needed to see in me.

(*She is crying.*)

You cry for yourself.

BEATRICE. I cry for you.

ADAM. For your own misery.

BEATRICE. For you, for you. I cry for you.

ADAM. I believe neither you nor your tears.

BEATRICE. Couldn't you see I whipped you from fear?

ADAM. Couldn't you see I retreated from fear?

BEATRICE. I don't know what I say.

ADAM. You know everything you say, only too well, you know everything.

BEATRICE. I exposed myself. Must I teach you such simple things? I'm so vulnerable and frightened.

ADAM. Frightened? You?

BEATRICE. Help me.

ADAM. I cannot.

BEATRICE. I give you my hand. Help me.

ADAM. I cannot.

BEATRICE. Let's make up. Like children. Let's do something silly. Climb a tree with me. Look at the moon with me. Like children, let's make up.

ADAM. If only I could. How well you know how to tempt me, don't you? Like children, make up, if only I could.

BEATRICE. Like children, Adam, a pact, like children.

ADAM. And then would come another moment and it would be as though no pact had ever existed and you would spit and spit and spit again, and then you would ask to be comforted and then again you'd spit and I'd be tossed from the right hand of your passion to the left hand of your venom and I cannot, I cannot, I cannot.

BEATRICE. Help me.

ADAM. I cannot.

(BEATRICE *now utters a terrifying moan that begins like a wail of despair but rises to a cry of anger – as though half way through her wail she realizes that it will have no effect and her plea will be unanswered.*

The cry ends abruptly. Both realize that the year has ended.

BEATRICE *moves to the chest of drawers and meticulously brings out the clothes to fold them ready for packing. Her calm is chilling.*)

BEATRICE. You know, there was nothing between us really, was there?

ADAM. Wasn't there?

BEATRICE. We weren't even really friends, were we?

ADAM. No?

BEATRICE. My husband always used to say to me I expected too much from people.

ADAM. What more?

BEATRICE. What more is there to say? Nothing happened. It was all play-acting. A girlish dream. I'm surprised at myself that I can still have girlish dreams. Nothing, nothing at all, nothing happened.

ADAM. No of course not, it was foolishness wasn't it? It's always foolish to try and know more than one person. To know more than one person is to betray them.

BEATRICE. On the contrary, to know only one person is to betray the world.

ADAM. Ah yes, the world.

BEATRICE. You can never be an island you know.

ADAM. Oh? Do you think that when the millennium comes there will not be lovers who grow weary of their sad girls, or that wives will not weep over empty beds? Even when Jerusalem is built friends will grow apart and mothers will mourn their sons growing old.

Do you want me to feel for starving children? I feel for them. Do you want me to protest at wars that go on in the mountains? I protest. But the heart has its private aches. You must allow the heart its private aches. Not all the good great causes in this world can stop me crying for a passing love.

(*Long Pause.*)

Beatrice, what do you remember most about him?

BEATRICE. What do I remember?

A long drive into the autumn countryside I remember. The astonishment we shared that trees and fields could burn with such colours. The tremendous blaze of dying hedges, the smouldering leaves, the discovery of these things.

I remember the plots against indifference, the ease with which we picked up each other's thoughts in our battles with the world, the language we gave each other. I remember the long walks into the long nights, the gratitude for his presence, my helplessness.

And I remember that when my father died in a far-off country I did not go to his side because I wanted to stay with *him*. And my father died alone – I was his favourite child. These things I remember. And you? Tell me the beautiful things you remember about her.

ADAM. Moments of music and silence and adoration I remember. The attention of her eyes. I remember the devotion of her limbs and the care she gave to everything she did for me from the tender binding of a present to the intimate cooking of a meal. I remember my cruelty and I remember her cruelty. These things.

I remember that we were not afraid to dance when we couldn't, to say we did not know things we should have known or admit each unimportant sin we had committed against each other. I remember that we were not afraid to laugh hysterically or to play with children or to grow old. I remember we were not afraid.

I remember my father dying and my holding his head in my hands and crying, 'Keep breathing, come on, don't give up Joe, don't stop Joe.' And my mother, through her tears, saying, 'You think he'll listen to you?' and smiling, and both of us sobbing and me wanting to run my hands continually over his eyes and cheeks and hair. These things I remember. Because moments like these remind me that time passes and time passing reminds me of sadness and waste and neglect and suffering. And I know in my heart that all those lovely moments of youth will not return. These things I remember, and because of it I'm a gentler person, it is easier for me to forgive and be forgiven. These things, Beatrice, these things I remember and know, just as you know and, for that reason, you will be gentler.

BEATRICE. I think I have an illness coming on. I'm feeling cold.

ADAM. Cold? Yes, it is cold isn't it! Shall we try and warm ourselves? Those dead leaves you swept up this morning – I'll start a fire with those.

(*He moves quickly outside and returns with a large armful of leaves which he throws into the grate.*)

BEATRICE. I don't know why I should be so cold.

ADAM. We'll soon be warm.

(*He tries to light the leaves. They only smoulder.*)

ADAM. They're damp.

BEATRICE. Autumn leaves. Dead. What did you expect?

(*He blows hard to bring them to flame.*)

ADAM. Burn, damn you, burn!

They won't light.

(ADAM *watches the feeble smoke.* BEATRICE *folds and folds and meticulously folds –*)

NOTES

The Apple Strudel

The process of making apple strudel is a very dramatic one and involves patience and experience. But actors learn to fence – why not to cook? The art lies in the pulling and stretching of the paste over a cloth covering the entire table until the paste is paper thin and hanging over the edges. Apples, raisins, nuts, cinnamon and sugar are now strewn along the length of the paste, which is rolled into a long pipe of strudel. This is done by pulling the cloth from under the paste which you then flick forward.

The problem is not to make holes in the pulling. Holes invariably appear and if they are small can be ignored; if they are large then they need to be patched up by tearing a piece off the edge.

The movement required is a beautiful one where the cook moves round and round the table pulling here, pulling there, not too much at a time, not too quickly, and most of the time using the back of his hand under the paste, drawing his hand towards him, rather than the fingers which would make holes. After a while the confident cook can flap the paste in order to help it stretch, rather as one does to a sheet on the bed in order to straighten it out. To watch this being done is really exciting and the best chefs clown while they do it.

When the paste has been stretched till the edges are hanging over four sides of the table the chef must move swiftly, or the paste, being so thin, will dry up. Obviously the thinner the paste becomes the more tense everyone is.

The paste is made of 1½ lbs flour, ¾ pt water, a pinch of salt, one egg and 2 teaspoonfuls of olive oil. It must be pummeled for a long time – in an automatic beater – until the mixture is smooth and pliable, just short of being tacky. The longer it is beaten the easier it is to stretch. It is left to rest for about twenty minutes, and then it is rolled out with a rolling pin into an oval shape about 18 ins by 9 ins, a quarter of an inch thick. Next a film of hot olive oil is rubbed gently over the entire surface and left to sink for thirty seconds; then the pulling begins.

None of this preparation is done in the play. The paste and ingredients are ready in time for the scene. Only the pulling and filling are acted.

Advice should be sought from a high-class pastry-cook.

The wind doth blow to-night my love and a few small drops of rain I never had but one true-love in cold grave she was lain.